Gallery Books
Editor: Peter Fallon

THE HOME PLACE

Brian Friel

THE
HOME
PLACE

Gallery Books

The Home Place
is first published
simultaneously in paperback
and in a clothbound edition
on the day of its première,
1 February 2005.

The Gallery Press
Loughcrew
Oldcastle
County Meath
Ireland

ISBN 1 85235 380 5 *paperback*
1 85235 381 3 *clothbound*

A CIP catalogue record for this book
is available from the British Library.

for Gary McKeone

Characters

MARGARET O'DONNELL
CON DOHERTY
SALLY CAVANAGH
JOHNNY MacLOONE
CHRISTOPHER GORE
DAVID GORE
DR RICHARD GORE
PERKINS
CLEMENT O'DONNELL
MARY SWEENEY
TOMMY BOYLE
MAISIE McLAUGHLIN

Set

Most of the action takes place on the unkempt lawn in front of The Lodge, the home of Christopher Gore and his son, David. The only house-interior we see is the breakfast room at right angles to the stage right. The French windows in this room open on to the lawn.

The house is approached by an (unseen) avenue off right. A crescent of trees encloses the entire house and lawn; it seems to press in on them. This meniscus is most dense down stage left. (Left and right from the point of view of the audience.)

Time and Place

Summer, 1878. Ballybeg, County Donegal, Ireland.

The Home Place was first performed in the Gate Theatre, Dublin, on Tuesday, 1 February 2005, with the following cast:

CHRISTOPHER GORE	Tom Courtenay
MARGARET O'DONNELL	Derbhle Crotty
DR RICHARD GORE	Nick Dunning
CON DOHERTY	Adam Fergus
JOHNNY MacLOONE	Michael Judd
PERKINS	Pat Kinevane
MARY SWEENEY	Brenda Larby
SALLY CAVANAGH	Laura Jane Laughlin
CLEMENT O'DONNELL	Barry McGovern
DAVID GORE	Hugh O'Conor
TOMMY BOYLE	Bill Ó Cléirigh/Kenneth McDonnell
MAISIE McLAUGHLIN	Leanna Duke/Ciara Lyons

Director	Adrian Noble
Set and Costume Designer	Peter McKintosh
Lighting Designer	Paul Pyant

ACT ONE

An early afternoon in late August. The sun is shining. The country-side is still.

MARGARET O'DONNELL enters right. She is in her early thirties; a handsome woman of intelligence and quiet conviction. She has been to the clothes line off right and carries a large laundry basket. She empties the clothes on to the lawn and begins separating the garments.

Suddenly, in the far distance, a school choir begins singing Thomas Moore's 'Oft in the Stilly Night'.

The music, at first scarcely audible, then slowly increasing in volume, is in opulent three-part harmony. The ethereal, sophisticated singing in this unlikely setting is wondrous.

The moment she becomes aware of the singing MARGARET stands motionless, enraptured. Then she is drawn as if mesmerized to the edge of the lawn, shields her eyes from the sun and looks down at the distant school stage right, the source of the music. She stands there for two full verses, absorbing the music, listening with her whole being, now and then silently mouthing the words of the song.

At the end of the first verse CON DOHERTY emerges suddenly and very briefly from the thicket left. He is in his mid-twenties: lean, keen features. He is soft spoken and very controlled. Everything he says and does is considered. The moment he sees MARGARET he melts back into the thicket.

SALLY CAVANAGH enters the breakfast room with her zinc bucket and shovel. She is in her early twenties; alert, saucy, astute. She goes to the French windows and for a few seconds observes MARGARET in her enchantment.

SALLY Will I clean out the grate now or — ?

> *She tails off because MARGARET is in a different world. She goes inside and begins lifting the ashes from the grate.*

The second verse of the song comes to an end:
MARGARET *is freed. She picks up her basket and goes towards the breakfast room. Just as she is about to go inside she catches a glimpse of a bird flying above the thicket stage left. She stops and looks for it. But it has vanished.*

She goes into the breakfast room and busies herself putting clean antimacassars on the couch and armchairs.

SALLY   Must be on the batter again.

MARGARET   What's that?

SALLY   Your da. He has the choir out in the playground. Do you not hear them?

MARGARET   (*Sniffing*) Some of these aren't properly aired.

SALLY   Showing off before the boss here; that's why he takes them outside; so that the sound will carry up here to The Lodge. Wasting his time: Mr Gore pays no heed to him.

MARGARET   (*Antimacassars*) Weren't ironed properly either.

SALLY   All the same no teacher ever made them sing as well as your aul' fella does — especially when he's on the batter. And the drunker he is the better they sing for him. Strange that, isn't it?

MARGARET   When you're finished there, put the chickens back into the henhouse.

SALLY   You told me to let them out.

MARGARET   The falcon's back. I'll have to get someone up to shoot him. The sergeant will do it for me.

SALLY   Did I hear Mr Gore leave very early this morning?

MARGARET   Before breakfast. David and himself. The memorial service for Lord Lifford.

SALLY   Doesn't seem all that long, does it?

MARGARET   This day four weeks exactly.

SALLY   That long? God, that was one dirty job. And no sign of the peelers lifting anybody either.

MARGARET   They will in time.

SALLY   I hope they do. Well maybe I do — God knows

they've questioned enough. Every man and boy in the parish must have been dragged in. All the same he was a bad beast, Lifford. The Lecher Lifford — wasn't he well named?

MARGARET Put a newspaper under that bucket, Sally.

SALLY I worked there for a whole year, you know. And I was only twelve at the time. Until my brother Manus came and took me away.

MARGARET You've told me.

SALLY If Lifford had been about that day, Manus would have given the bugger a hammering he wouldn't have forgot. Listen!

Stopped (*music*). Your da's probably nipped across to the pub. In all the four years I was at school, he never let me into the choir — just because my name was Cavanagh. 'Never met a Cavanagh who wasn't a crow.'

MARGARET Our visitors are leaving this evening. You can change the sheets in the guest room; and the towels.

SALLY You must have been in his choir in your day?

MARGARET I was.

SALLY 'Course you were. Weren't you his pet? (*Pause*) Do you never go home now at all, Maggie?

MARGARET You'll need to dig some potatoes for the dinner. And take down the curtains in the sitting room and soak them in cold water. And clean the windows in the pantry.

SALLY Anything else, Maggie?

MARGARET Don't forget to put the chickens inside.

> MARGARET *goes into the house.* SALLY *finishes her job at the grate and goes out to the lawn to empty the ashes off stage right.* CON *emerges from the thicket left.*

CON (*Whispers*) Sally!

> *She looks round, alarmed. She sees him. A second*

of unease: is MARGARET *watching? Now she dashes to the right and flings the bucket recklessly into the trees. Then, brushing down her dress, she crosses quickly to* CON. *They talk in whispers.*

SALLY Are you off your head? You shouldn't be jouking about up here!

CON That's a great welcome.

SALLY When did you get back from England?

CON At three this morning.

SALLY God, it was the longest two weeks ever! What were you at over there?

CON Meeting people; travelling around; addressing small groups.

SALLY That must have been rare fun.

CON Has to be done.

SALLY Just you and that queer bucko from Dungannon — Stephen — ?

He puts a finger on her lips.

CON Shhh.

SALLY And why are you dodging about up here?

CON To see you, Sally.

SALLY I'm sure! You look exhausted, Con.

CON The two visitors are still here?

SALLY Leaving today.

CON What time?

SALLY This evening, I think. Why?

CON They're going straight to the Aran Islands?

SALLY How do you know that? What are you up to, Con?

CON Look at that anxious face.

Another figure emerges from the thicket and stands beside CON. JOHNNY MACLOONE *is a very large man in his sixties.*

SALLY Who's he? Who are you?

CON He's from Meendoran.

SALLY What's your name?

CON Johnny MacLoone.

SALLY What are you doing up here?

CON He's with me.

SALLY Will you let the dummy speak!

JOHNNY Mind your mouth, girl.

SALLY He's not a dummy!

JOHNNY Watch yourself, woman.

CON He's a friend of mine, Sally.

SALLY What's all this about?

CON Will you meet me tonight?

> MARGARET *has returned to the breakfast room with fresh cushion covers.*

MARGARET Sally!

SALLY Bitch. (*Calls*) Coming! (*To* CON) Where?

CON Behind Roarty's forge.

SALLY When?

CON I have to meet somebody at eight. Ten o'clock?

SALLY Jesus, Con, you're not up to something stupid, are you?

CON If you're not there at ten, I won't wait.

> *She gives him a quick, flirtatious kiss on the cheek.*

SALLY Yes, you will. (*To* JOHNNY) 'Bye, chatterbox.

> *She runs back to the breakfast room. The two men merge into the thicket.*

I left the bucket of ashes sitting here, didn't I?

MARGARET Were you talking to somebody?

SALLY What's that?

MARGARET Who were you talking to, Sally?

SALLY Con Doherty from Ballybeg.

MARGARET I thought that wastrel had left the country?

SALLY Comes and goes.

MARGARET What's he doing trespassing up here?

SALLY Snaring rabbits maybe. How would I know?

MARGARET He knows very well that's not permitted on these lands.

SALLY Cousin of yours, Maggie, isn't he? Maybe he thinks that entitles him?

MARGARET He's very wrong then.

SALLY Or maybe like a lot of others about here he believes he's entitled to walk these lands any time he wants.

MARGARET And like a lot of others it would fit him better to do a decent day's work instead of going around whispering defiance into the ears of stupid young fools. Whatever ugly activity he's involved in, we want none of it here. And spread a table-cloth on the lawn. We'll have afternoon tea outside today.

SALLY Will 'we'? You'd do anything to be one of the toffs, Maggie, wouldn't you?

MARGARET Any more cheek like that from you, miss, and you'll be back down below herding your one cow.

SALLY (*Exiting*) And Con Doherty's no wastrel!

> SALLY *goes out to the lawn again. She glances quickly at the thicket — no sign of the two men. She goes off right.*
>
> CHRISTOPHER GORE *enters from the house. He is in his late fifties; effusive, bumbling, obstinate. Unnoticed by* MARGARET *he moves up behind her and catches her by the shoulder.*

CHRISTOPHER What's in that head of yours?

MARGARET You're back! I didn't hear the car.

CHRISTOPHER Tell me what's in there.

> *She extricates herself deftly.*

MARGARET   Not a thing, Christopher. Did you have lunch?
CHRISTOPHER You're so elegant in that dress. Everything you wear you adorn.
MARGARET   It's sixteen years old at least.
CHRISTOPHER Really beautiful.
MARGARET   For heaven's sake I can scarcely squeeze into it. Is David with you?
CHRISTOPHER Mooning about somewhere — I don't know — in the stables maybe.
MARGARET   And how was the memorial service?
CHRISTOPHER Subdued. No, it was awful, just awful.
MARGARET   A big turn-out?
CHRISTOPHER Eleven of us.
MARGARET   Is that all?
CHRISTOPHER Huddled together; talking in whispers.
MARGARET   There were no locals?
CHRISTOPHER What am I, Margaret?
MARGARET   What I mean is —
CHRISTOPHER No, only us. Frightened — terrified, for God's sake: which of us is next on the list.
MARGARET   You know there is no list. It was an isolated crime, Christopher. How's Penelope bearing up?
CHRISTOPHER Valiantly, it would appear. Quite demented, I suspect. And alone now in that enormous barracks of a house. She'll be seventy next week, Penny.
MARGARET   Do they know yet what happened?
CHRISTOPHER He was going to oversee the eviction of one of his tenants.
MARGARET   Who?
CHRISTOPHER Some welsher. Does it matter? The police car was in front and his car fell behind — they think his horses had been lamed deliberately.
MARGARET   Were they?
CHRISTOPHER Probably. Roarty, the blacksmith, is under suspicion. Anyhow they shot his driver and then they dragged poor old Lifford out of the car and battered in his skull with a granite rock.
MARGARET   God, Christopher —

CHRISTOPHER Penny told the story to each of us in turn with the same patient detail. The top mother-of-pearl button was ripped from his waistcoat. In his left hand he was clutching the fob of his watch — a violet amethyst he brought back years ago from his time in the Congo. And he must have put up a ferocious fight because in his right hand he had a clump of his attacker's hair. Black hair. Curly.

MARGARET Oh my God —

CHRISTOPHER She told the story to each of us in turn with the same patient detail and with such pride in his courage that the faded green eyes suddenly gleamed again. As if all the humiliations — dammit, the physical violence — the old bastard inflicted on her for over fifty years had never happened. And she was the pert and intrepid little Penny Pasco again who came over here from Devonshire all those years ago, full of joy and expectation. Such a gallant woman she is. There isn't a list, Margaret, is there?

MARGARET Of course there isn't.

CHRISTOPHER Of course there isn't. Just an isolated, barbarous incident.

MARGARET Lifford was a very ugly creature, Christopher. Even his own people hated him.

CHRISTOPHER I didn't. I never liked him, but I didn't hate him. And I love this place so much, Margaret. This is the only home I've ever known.

MARGARET I know that.

CHRISTOPHER At this time of year Penny used to spend days on end here, picking fruit; herself and Lucy, rest in peace. Like sisters — Before the walled garden went to seed. (*Suddenly brisk*) Rise above, Father always said — rise above — rise above. Where are our guests?

MARGARET Gone for a walk.

CHRISTOPHER Yes?

MARGARET Richard wanted to see the ruins of the old

Cistercian monastery.

CHRISTOPHER He's entranced by you is Cousin Richard.

MARGARET Christopher!

CHRISTOPHER Sat gazing at you all through dinner last night. Don't pretend you didn't notice.

Again he holds her shoulders. Again she eludes him.

MARGARET The man was drunk, Christopher.

CHRISTOPHER He was a little, wasn't he?

MARGARET And I really got an earful of your boyhood escapades in Kent.

CHRISTOPHER My God, you did, didn't you! Sorry. So boring, I know. And the truth is I *hated* being shipped over to the home place every damned summer. Father thought it would make Richard and me close friends.

MARGARET And did it?

CHRISTOPHER D'you know what I discovered last night? All those memories of Kent — they almost made me homesick. What do you make of him?

MARGARET A little pompous maybe?

CHRISTOPHER He is a bore and a snob and utterly graceless and I have a very soft spot for him. Must have something to do with India itself: everyone who does even a short service there comes home gross. Father was convinced the climate did it.

MARGARET I didn't think he was gross. Just so caught up in his own world. The confirmed bachelor, isn't he?

CHRISTOPHER Getting married.

MARGARET Richard?

CHRISTOPHER Next year.

MARGARET He's not!

CHRISTOPHER Didn't tell me until you had retired — 'Not before the staff' — that old snob thing in him. Edith Something-or-Other. A doctor, too. Went with him to the Outer Hebrides last spring on one of those silly expeditions of his — ethnology? — anthropology? — anthropometry? — whatever. He loves tossing out those big words. I didn't understand a bit of it, I think. Did you?

MARGARET   Not at all.

CHRISTOPHER   You kept nodding your head very intelligently all through dinner.

MARGARET   I was falling asleep.

CHRISTOPHER   Shame on you. If I understand him at all, what the anthropologist does is study a people's distinctive characteristics and then classify those characteristics according to their race.

MARGARET   That's the ethnologist, I think.

CHRISTOPHER   You're right. The classifying. That's why he spent three summers on the Aran Islands — just measuring people's heads, for God's sake.

MARGARET   That's the anthropometrist, I think.

CHRISTOPHER   You're right. The measuring. He's trying to prove — isn't he? — that every race has its own distinctive physical characteristics: distinctive height; colour of eyes; shape of skull; their nigrescence —

MARGARET   Their what?

CHRISTOPHER   Nigrescence. How black is their hair, their eyes, their complexion. You *were* asleep!

MARGARET   You're making this up, Christopher. And you weren't altogether sober either.

CHRISTOPHER   Thank you. Now what the anthropometrist does is make a detailed survey of the physical features of maybe a thousand people; and what emerges is a portrait of a distinctive ethnic group.

MARGARET   That's the anthropologist, I think.

CHRISTOPHER   You're wrong. Physical features. (*He raises his face; finger on chin; mock heroic*) Unmistakably Anglo-Saxon. (*Points to her*) And that quite elegant creature? Unmistakably Celt.

MARGARET   So what — then what?

CHRISTOPHER   Aha! Then we come to the clever part. Because what Cousin Richard believes is that behind that physical portrait, beneath that exquisite

Celtic appearance, there is a psychological portrait. And if only we could read that it would tell us how intelligent that tribe is, how stupid, how cunning, how ambitious. How faithful, for heaven's sake.

MARGARET He can't believe that!

Pause. He considers this.

CHRISTOPHER Can't. Can he? Plain silly. (*Softly*) Silly man in many ways, Cousin Richard. And you're right: we weren't altogether sober. You look so beautiful when you're mystified.

MARGARET I'm trying to imagine Richard married!

CHRISTOPHER Whatever about his ridiculous theories he did say something very perceptive to me last night. I was carrying the old goat up to bed when he suddenly announced, 'Edith is a splendid woman. But what an absolutely delicious creature your chatelaine is. I do envy you.' Meant it, too.

Again he reaches for her hand. Again she eludes him. Pause.

That service was so — so disturbing. I need a drink.

She drifts out to the lawn. He pours a drink. She looks down towards the school. He joins her.

We're invited to the wedding. Yes, you too. Now that's a big gesture. But I said we'd be caught up here with the harvest. You don't want to go all the way to the home place in Kent just to see old Dick and Edith being spliced, would you? But you're so right: she'll have her hands full squeezing his old bachelor habits out of him.

MARGARET What's a chatelaine, Christopher?

CHRISTOPHER She's welcome to that job. A chatelaine? Mistress of a large house, I suppose.

MARGARET Is that what I am?

CHRISTOPHER Bloomers! That's her name! Edith Bloomers! (*Laughs*) Miss Bloomers won't regret shedding that name. Not that a doctor called Gore is much better, is it?

SALLY enters right, brandishing her bucket.

SALLY Found it! Look! In the middle of the black-currant bushes.

CHRISTOPHER Sorry?

SALLY The bucket!

CHRISTOPHER Yes?

SALLY That's where you hid it, Mr Gore, isn't it?

CHRISTOPHER Did I?

SALLY Yes! In the bushes!

CHRISTOPHER Why would I hide your bucket in the black-currant bushes?

SALLY Just the kind of trick you would play, isn't it?

CHRISTOPHER (*To* MARGARET) The cheek of that child! How dare you, missy!

SALLY You'll have to think up a better hiding place.

She goes into the house.

CHRISTOPHER What a saucy little imp she is. (*He catches* MARGARET *by the shoulders*) That's what I love about her.

Again she eludes him.

Something the matter?

MARGARET She's an insolent madam.

CHRISTOPHER So were you when you came here first.

MARGARET At fourteen years of age?

CHRISTOPHER Alright — ambitious.

MARGARET I was terrified, Christopher!

CHRISTOPHER Joking — joking. Actually I *do* remember your first day here in The Lodge.

MARGARET You do not.

CHRISTOPHER Vividly. Your father presented you very formally to Lucy, rest in peace. 'Margaret, my first born and my prime chorister. Be mindful of her.'

MARGARET Typical Father — 'Be mindful'! Was he sober?

CHRISTOPHER He was so proud. Why wouldn't he be?

He catches her hand and raises it to his lips. As he does, DAVID *comes round the side of the house. He is about thirty; a hesitant, uncertain young man. All three are embarrassed.*

DAVID I've mixed the lime and water, Father.

CHRISTOPHER (*Feigned puzzlement*) Well done. What are you talking about?

DAVID The white-wash you wanted.

CHRISTOPHER Why did I want white-wash?

DAVID To put a mark on the trees you are going to cut down.

CHRISTOPHER I know I'm being terribly tiresome. What trees, David?

DAVID You said you wanted to thin out the trees at the side there (*left*).

MARGARET You discussed it at length yesterday morning, Christopher.

CHRISTOPHER The doomed trees! Of course! We must do that.

DAVID So — Whenever you're ready —

CHRISTOPHER You mean we mark them now, David? You mean at this very moment? Could our little task wait until this evening?

DAVID Yes — yes — that's —

CHRISTOPHER Perhaps after our guests have gone?

DAVID Of course. Yes.

CHRISTOPHER But only if that's agreeable to you?

MARGARET (*Quickly, sharply*) Have you both had something to eat?

CHRISTOPHER Penny foddered us handsomely, thank you kindly.

23

The doomed trees later. Must get out of these rags.

As he goes into the house

DAVID I was wondering, Father —

CHRISTOPHER Yes?

DAVID I just wondered is this perhaps the right moment for Richard to carry out his — whatever it is Richard intends doing?

CHRISTOPHER No idea what you're talking about, David.

DAVID Just that I got a sense in the village recently — you felt it at the service today, too — just that everybody seems to be a bit — I don't know — vigilant? — on edge?

CHRISTOPHER For heaven's sake, who could object to Richard's silly tabulations? Nothing to worry about. Good to be vigilant. (*Softly*) By the way what's the name of his clerk fellow? Tomkins? — Watkins?

MARGARET Perkins.

CHRISTOPHER Perkins — the parrot!

MARGARET He told me this morning his grandmother came from Wicklow.

CHRISTOPHER (*Parrot voice*) 'Grandmother came from Wicklow.'

MARGARET (*Admonishing finger*) Christopher!

CHRISTOPHER And just watch him, Margaret: he has a lascivious eye on our little Sally.

He goes into the house; and immediately DAVID *embraces* MARGARET.

DAVID Let me hold you, Maggie.

MARGARET Shhh — careful, David.

DAVID I haven't held you since breakfast-time.

MARGARET What did you hear in the village?

DAVID I've got the most unbelievably good news.

MARGARET David —

DAVID Devised a most audacious plan for us. No more

secrecy. No more tip-toeing about.

MARGARET Tell me what you heard.

DAVID Just a restlessness — a whiff of unease — that Lifford business — nothing to do with us. Promise — nothing at all.

The new scheme is simple and it is daring and I am hugely, inordinately proud of it. In fact it is a plan touched by genius.

MARGARET Genius?

DAVID Genius.

Pause.

MARGARET Well?

DAVID We'll run away to Glasgow!

MARGARET (*Flatly*) Glasgow.

DAVID We'll go to Derry next Saturday to buy some fencing-posts, ho-ho-ho. We'll get the boat there that night. And on Sunday morning there will be magnificent Glasgow and a glorious new life spread out before us.

MARGARET And what will you do in Glasgow?

DAVID What all the men from around here do: labour on one of those enormous Scottish farms! I'll be a tattie-hoker, for God's sake! And when the harvest is over we'll move to Edinburgh and I'll give 'cello lessons. Things may be tight for a time but I have saved enough money to tide us over for a fortnight at least. And we can live frugally — two rooms, one room. It'll be no hardship for you — you're so adaptable.

MARGARET (*Wearily*) You can't 'run away' to Glasgow, David.

DAVID Why can't we?

MARGARET And one day's labouring would kill you. And you'd suffocate in one room. And you haven't played the 'cello for twenty years. And you don't even know what tattie-hoking means!

DAVID Of course I know. It means — hoking tatties.

MARGARET (*Gently*) It's not really a wonderful scheme, is it?

Pause.

DAVID I have a fall-back.

MARGARET I am right, amn't I?

DAVID Selberawawa.

MARGARET What?

DAVID In Kenya. North-East of Nairobi. A nephew of Mother's has a huge estate there. Tristram Brooke. His home place is in Warwickshire.

MARGARET North-East of Nairobi.

DAVID Exactly! Tristram farms goats. Exports thousands of skins every year.

MARGARET And what would you do in Selberawawa?

DAVID Wash the skins. Herd the goats. Make cheese. Tristram has asked me out a dozen times. He'd be thrilled to have us. He has the most enormous farm; thousands of acres. And an entire tribe of two hundred natives are tenants on this estate: wonderful workers, the sweetest people. And he's married to a Kikuyu warrior — the gentlest woman imaginable. She speaks only Bantu but she's picking up some English words — in a Warwickshire accent! It will be a wonderful adventure and a wonderful new beginning. I love you so much, Maggie.

MARGARET You've got to stop talking about running away.

DAVID So very much. Oh, God.

MARGARET Your family has been here in The Lodge for centuries. This is your home.

DAVID With Father? Who keeps humiliating me?

MARGARET And you're going to be here for the rest of your life.

DAVID How can you make a prediction like that? You know what the locals call us? — the Lodgers. And you see Father's cruelties. Of course you do. I think he humiliates me because he's in love with you.

MARGARET David.

DAVID You know he is.

MARGARET He's a very lonely man.

DAVID Can't hide it any more.

MARGARET The only people he meets around here are —

DAVID Oh yes — he's in love with you.

MARGARET That's ridiculous, David.

DAVID And I always hoped that maybe you could come to love me. For as long as I can remember that's what I hoped. Even away back when I was playing the 'cello! That was my hope.

MARGARET I do, David.

DAVID Maybe not now, not at this very moment, as Father might say; but in time — maybe in time.

MARGARET Yes.

DAVID And that some time, some day to come, maybe you would consider marrying me.

MARGARET Yes, I do.

DAVID Do what?

MARGARET Love you.

DAVID You don't.

MARGARET Yes.

DAVID No, you don't, Margaret.

MARGARET Yes.

DAVID Me?

MARGARET You.

DAVID Oh my God.

Pause. He stares at her.

You never said that before.

MARGARET You don't listen to me.

Pause.

DAVID Say it again.

MARGARET I love you.

Pause.

DAVID No, you don't.

MARGARET I love you, David.

Pause. Now he is convinced.

DAVID Yes, I'm listening! Yes, you do! Oh my God! This is just awful! I'll be a superb goat-skinner! I'll be a brilliant 'cellist. I'll hoke tatties as they were never hoked before! I'll treat you like a queen.
MARGARET Keep your voice —
DAVID Yes — yes — yes — yes — yes!

As he releases this exuberant cry he catches her in his arms and dances with her and sings at the top of his voice. At some point during this singing/dancing, SALLY enters the breakfast room to pick up a tray. She observes them for a few seconds and then exits.

DAVID 'The young May moon is beaming, love — '
MARGARET David —
DAVID 'The glow-worm's lamp is gleaming, love — '
MARGARET Your father will hear —
DAVID 'How sweet to rove/Through Morna's grove? While the drowsy world is dreaming, love.'
MARGARET David, please, David —
DAVID 'Then awake. The heavens look bright, my dear — '
MARGARET My head's spinning, David —
DAVID 'Tis never too late for delight, my dear./And the best of all ways/To lengthen our days — '
MARGARET David — David — David —
DAVID 'Is to steal a few hours from the night, my dear.'

The song/dance ends embarrassedly with the entry right of RICHARD and PERKINS. As they enter RICHARD removes his Panama hat and hands it and his cane to PERKINS.

RICHARD is a bachelor in his sixties. A man of resolute habits and Victorian confidence. He is

28

*aware that this is how he is seen and it gives
him sly pleasure to play up to that stereotype.*

*PERKINS, his personal assistant, is in his forties.
Like his employer he knows he plays a role; and
he, too, enjoys playing it.*

RICHARD Take these indoors, Perkins.

PERKINS Indoors, Sir.

RICHARD And fetch me the box of instruments.

PERKINS Where is it positioned, Sir?

RICHARD Beside the longcase clock in the hall.

PERKINS The longcase clock. Certainly, Sir.

PERKINS *goes into the house.*

DAVID (*Extravagantly*) You are very welcome back,
Richard. Very good to see you again.

RICHARD Yes? (*To* MARGARET) You're right. Well worth a
visit, that monastery. When does it date from?

MARGARET Seventh century.

RICHARD And what a huge expanse of buildings! It must
have been a miniature city!

MARGARET And an important centre of learning, it seems.
Some great documents were reproduced there.

RICHARD (*To* DAVID) How was the service?

DAVID Dismal, I suppose.

RICHARD Savage business. (*Calls*) Perkins! Thugs, whoever
did it.

PERKINS (*Off*) Sir?

RICHARD We'll require a table and chairs.

PERKINS (*Off*) Table and chairs. Yes, Sir.

RICHARD (*To* MARGARET) Is that possible?

MARGARET I'll get them.

RICHARD (*Calls*) And the camera.

PERKINS (*Off*) Camera, Sir.

RICHARD We'll hold the clinic out here — with your bless-
ing. Can't have the hoplites tramping all over
your carpets, can we? Did I hear singing somewhere in the distance?

DAVID   That's the local school choir.

RICHARD   Very fetching, too.

DAVID   That is the most famous choir in all Donegal. Margaret's father is the teacher.

RICHARD   (*To* MARGARET) Bravo!

DAVID   Clement O'Donnell. Remarkable man.

MARGARET   On a calm day the sound carries up here.

DAVID   It really is magnificent, Richard. Margaret was in it in her day, too.

MARGARET   A long time ago. Tea is coming. Richard?

RICHARD   Bless you.

MARGARET   I'll tell Christopher you're home.

MARGARET *goes into the house.*

DAVID   If you were here for another day I'd get Clement to give you a concert.

RICHARD   Delicious creature that, isn't she? Urged your father last night to wed her. No doubt he's bedding her but marriage is what he needs. Been a widower far too long.

DAVID   What did he say?

RICHARD   What *did* he say? (*Laughs*) Can't remember. We were both a little squishy. (*Softly*) Wouldn't be inhibited about marrying down, would he?

DAVID   Do you mean somebody who — ?

RICHARD   Shouldn't be. That could be well worth a flutter.

SALLY *emerges with a tray of tea things. She spreads a cloth on the grass.* DAVID *helps her.*

RICHARD   We're not going to be fed again, are we?

DAVID   Would you prefer a drink, Richard?

RICHARD   No, no. (*To* SALLY) What have you got for us?

SALLY   Tea, Sir.

RICHARD   Good!

SALLY   And sandwiches.

RICHARD   Splendid!

SALLY   And shortbread.

RICHARD I'm a slave to shortbread. (*To* DAVID) She's out to subvert me.

SALLY I'm what, Sir?

DAVID Thank you, Sally. That's fine.

RICHARD Your father has dragooned some specimens for me?

DAVID He did say something about —

RICHARD Small sampling will suffice. Our major work is on the Aran Islands. You've been there?

DAVID Never. (*To* SALLY) These look good (*sandwiches*).

SALLY Cold beef. Specially for you.

DAVID You're a dote.

RICHARD We're heading there this evening. Why don't you come with us?

DAVID I'd like to, Richard. But Father and I have to thin out those trees.

RICHARD An awesome place inhabited by a truly remarkable tribe. You must see them. Handsome, wild, courteous, vengeful.

DAVID Why vengeful?

RICHARD (*Whispers*) Irish.

DAVID (*Laughs*) Richard!

RICHARD Extraordinarily long faces and black eyes. And of course addicted to the most extravagant superstitions.

DAVID Richard!

RICHARD A primeval people really. Sally, isn't it?

SALLY Sally it is, Sir.

RICHARD You ministered to us magnificently last night, Sally.

SALLY You enjoyed yourself, Sir?

RICHARD A little too well perhaps?

SALLY You, Sir? Never!

RICHARD You have an artful one there, David.

DAVID Are you artful, Sally?

SALLY What do you mean by that?

RICHARD See! Bred in the bone. Excellent (*shortbread*). Oh yes; they were the original Firbolgs, the Aran people, according to Celtic tradition; and for thousands of years untouched by outside influences. Until Cromwell put a garrison of our men there and of course they were married with the natives and within a couple of generations the Firbolg integrity was vitiated. Well done!

This to CHRISTOPHER *and* PERKINS *who emerge with a table and chairs, a box of instruments and a camera.*

CHRISTOPHER Where do you want this (*table*), cousin?

RICHARD Just place it there. Thank you. (*To* PERKINS) Mind artful Sally's dishes. And a chair there and there. Careful with that camera, Perkins.

PERKINS Careful, Sir.

RICHARD For God's sake, man, give it to me.

DAVID I'll take it.

RICHARD Thank you, David. Very special tool that. We've taken hundreds of photographs of the Aran tribe and everybody gets a picture of himself as a reward. Photographs are our glass beads.

DAVID Isn't that a little crude?

CHRISTOPHER Richard crude? Never!

RICHARD I promise you that the natives are thrilled by them. Send them as special trophies to their relatives in America. (*To* PERKINS) Instrument box?

PERKINS Instrument box, Sir.

RICHARD Well, place it on the table, man.

PERKINS On the table, Sir.

RICHARD Now, Chris, all that's missing are our specimens. How many do you expect?

CHRISTOPHER As many as turn up, I suppose.

RICHARD (*To* DAVID) He keeps lapsing into these Irish idioms. (*To* CHRISTOPHER) These people are your tenants, aren't they?

CHRISTOPHER Some of them, yes. Perhaps all of them.

RICHARD They are or they are not?

CHRISTOPHER That depends on who volunteers, doesn't it? (*Laughs*) If anybody does.

RICHARD And when can we expect them?

CHRISTOPHER They were told to be here at three o'clock. But — bless them — they're very cavalier about that kind of discipline.

RICHARD So some few — who may or may not be your tenants — may or may not present themselves but at a time we can't determine, can we? That's all for now, Perkins. We may or may not need you presently.

PERKINS May or may not, Sir. (*Softly to* SALLY) Your shortbread is breathtaking.

SALLY Say that again — quickly.

PERKINS Your short breath is bread — Your short —

SALLY Good try.

PERKINS *exits.*

CHRISTOPHER You're becoming a martinet, Dick.

RICHARD And you're going native. Next thing you'll marry an Irish woman and whatever is still Kentish in you will be extinguished. (*To* DAVID) Up to you to see that doesn't happen.

CHRISTOPHER Or perhaps the very lucky Irish woman will become a little Kentish.

RICHARD You're being flippant; but that can happen. Last season I was at an archery meeting in Kilkenny and the South Mayo Agricultural Show. And at both events the upper Irish classes there have lighter-coloured hair and lighter-coloured eyes than the lower Irish classes. And why? A generous infusion of English blood into the new landed classes and the new professional classes — people who were mere cotters or tribesmen a few generations back.

CHRISTOPHER You mean they were uglier then?

RICHARD I'm talking about evolution working progressively for once.

CHRISTOPHER I'm not rising to that bait.

RICHARD (*Innocently, to* DAVID) What bait?

33

DAVID   And I'm not getting involved.

CHRISTOPHER   Let me see if any volunteers have arrived. They may be loitering down the avenue. (*As he exits right*) But then again — (*Laughs*)

RICHARD   Pity to see Kent vanish — if he does marry her. Bigger pity though if she were to be diluted. Wouldn't it?

DAVID   Time for a drink, I think.

He goes into the breakfast room.

RICHARD   A conundrum for you, David. Guess when this was written. 'There are three races of people in Ireland. There are the Spanish in Kerry and Limerick. They are tall and thin with dark eyes and lank, black hair. There are the Scots in the North; a tribe of angular people with long visage and blue-grey eyes. And there are the people of Norwegian ancestry in County Wexford.' Well — when?

DAVID   (*Emerging*) Sorry?

RICHARD   A hundred years ago! By an English agriculturalist called Young. And he concludes, 'The rest of the kingdom is made up of mongrels.'

DAVID   Us?

RICHARD   But the interesting thing is that Young — who never once measured a head or facial features, never drew up a chart of stature or nigrescence — there he was in 1780 commenting astutely on the physical characteristics of Irish tribes; and then — then deducing from those physical features how those tribes might behave. Have you ever looked closely at the people of Cavan?

DAVID   Not for some days, Dick.

RICHARD   Smooth features, large limbs, with much broader hands than other Irishmen. Taciturn creatures and by no means unworthy subjects. But curiously — curiously a people given to deviousness and perfidy. Now — why is that?

DAVID   Their hands are too broad?

RICHARD   Is it because they are descended from the Tuatha Dé Danann, as my colleague William Wilde insists? You know Wilde — father of that execrable aesthete creature. And Wilde is a considerable anthropologist. Or look at the people of Wexford.

DAVID   The Norwegians.

RICHARD   Exactly. Of Scandinavian aspect. Industrious; peaceable, exemplary farmers. And yet those same peaceable people were the very backbone of the '98 Rebellion and most barbarous in their prosecution of it. Now, David, can you imagine how different our history would be if treason like that could be anticipated? (*To* SALLY) Come here, child.

DAVID   What's your point, Richard?

RICHARD   Come here — come here — come here! I'm not going to ravish you!

SALLY goes reluctantly to him. He grips her chin in his right hand and forces her head back.

Consider this, David. Head long and narrow, with slight parietal bulging. Small eyes. Blue-grey irises. Nose slightly aquiline in profile and —

SALLY   Sir, you're hurting me!

RICHARD   Not a bit. Well developed chin. Black hair. Complexion clear and ruddy. And you'll find sight and hearing extraordinarily keen. In short — typical of the Celtic breed in Donegal.

He slaps her bottom in dismissal.

Back to the paddock.

DAVID   Have a cup of tea yourself, Sally.

RICHARD   Yes, yes, we have become very expert at drawing up our charts and our tables and our dreary pedigrees. But the big prize still eludes us, David.

35

DAVID Does it?

RICHARD Isn't it just possible that that combination of black hair and strong chin and clear complexion are much more than the haphazard confluence of physical accidents? That they constitute an ethnic code we can't yet decipher? That they are signposts to an enormous vault of genetic information that is only just beyond the reach of our understanding? Are they saying to us — these physical features — if only we could hear them — are they whispering to us: Crack our code and we will reveal to you how a man thinks, what his character traits are, his loyalties, his vices, his entire intellectual architecture. Because if we could interpret that hair and chin and complexion, would it tell us that artful Sally could be — a designer of a brilliant canal system, a compulsive liar, a new Florence Nightingale, a rebel at heart maybe, maybe even a traitor? Is that the concealed Sally?

MARGARET *comes out with fresh tea.*

(*Softly*) If we could break into that vault, David, we wouldn't control just an empire. We would rule the entire universe.

MARGARET Is what the concealed Sally?

DAVID Richard is of the opinion that if we —

RICHARD Not an opinion. No, no. Tomorrow's exact science. This is a feast, Margaret.

MARGARET Just a snack. (*To* SALLY) You forgot the serviettes. On the kitchen table.

SALLY *goes off.*

More tea, Richard?

RICHARD If you would be so kind.

MARGARET David?

DAVID Let me help you.

RICHARD   May we include Perkins?

MARGARET   Of course.

RICHARD   Just to keep him genial. (*Calls*) Perkins! Tea!

PERKINS   Tea, Sir. Coming.

SALLY *returns with the serviettes.*

MARGARET   How does he always manage to be within ear-shot?

RICHARD   (*Whispers*) Always eavesdropping.

MARGARET   (*Laughs*) Richard!

RICHARD   Obsessed with curiosity. Characteristic of all the Norfolk Fens people. Also tiny feet and remarkably large hat-size.

MARGARET   I think you're secretly laughing at us all, Richard.

RICHARD   Never!

SALLY *hands the serviettes to* MARGARET.

MARGARET   They're not for me, are they? Hand them round.

RICHARD   Deeply suspicious, too, your Fens man. But straight as a die and faithful as a Gurkha.

CHRISTOPHER *enters right.*

CHRISTOPHER   Nobody so far, I'm afraid. Probably some confusion about the time.

RICHARD   It's now three-thirty.

CHRISTOPHER   We'll give them another few minutes. Or so. Well done, Margaret. I'm parched. Thank you, Sally (*serviette*). I said three o'clock explicitly. Your watch is fast, Dick.

SALLY   Will I take a look?

CHRISTOPHER   If you would. Can't imagine what can have happened.

SALLY *exits right.* PERKINS *comes out of the house.*

RICHARD	Tea, Perkins?
PERKINS	Tea, Sir. Grateful.
MARGARET	Shortbread, Richard?
RICHARD	Did you make them yourself?
MARGARET	This morning.
RICHARD	Take two if I may. (*To* PERKINS) Is your hatband twenty-four inches?
PERKINS	Twenty-four-and-a-half, Sir.
RICHARD	(*To* MARGARET) Pure Fens.
MARGARET	You *are* laughing at us.
RICHARD	(*Whispers*) And look at the feet — weeny.
DAVID	Have you ever been to Kenya, Richard?
RICHARD	Never. Why do you ask?
DAVID	Just that Mother has a distant cousin there. (*To* CHRISTOPHER) Tristram. Tristram Brooke. We hear from him every Christmas.
CHRISTOPHER	Do we?
DAVID	Occasionally.
CHRISTOPHER	Tristram Brooke.
DAVID	The home place is in Warwickshire. Tristram lives North-East of Nairobi. In Selberawawa.
CHRISTOPHER	In — ? You've just made that name up, David!
MARGARET	(*Quickly*) We have sandwiches and biscuits here, too — who's for what?
RICHARD	Commend the shortbread. (*To* DAVID) Kenya? Like to go there. Our crowd out there say it's a delightful place. And peaceful.

CLEMENT O'DONNELL *enters right. Blustery; breathless; compelled to talk when he knows he should be quiet. And now fuelled by drink. He could be a vagrant.*

CLEMENT	Forgive me — I know — I know — I'm an intruder and interrupting a happy domestic assemblage, a congress of family and friends — I'm very conscious of that. And for my graceless invasion, Mr Christopher, I do offer you my most —

CHRISTOPHER It's Clement O'Donnell!
CLEMENT It is, too. And not clad for polite company. But then I've known three generations of the Gore family; and The Lodge has always been a house of tolerance and grace. So I do have a confidence that my present condition will be afforded the indulgence this family has always —
CHRISTOPHER (*Holds up a silencing hand*) O'Donnell!
CLEMENT Sir.
CHRISTOPHER You know very well you are welcome in this house day or night.
CLEMENT I thank you for that.
CHRISTOPHER Now. You've never met my cousin, Richard, have you? Clement O'Donnell — Doctor Gore.
CLEMENT Honoured, Sir.
CHRISTOPHER Richard's from the home place in Kent. And his assistant, Perkins.
CLEMENT Mr Perkins. Delighted.
PERKINS Delighted.
DAVID How are you, Clement?
CLEMENT Ah — Master David!
DAVID Very good to see you, Clement.
CLEMENT Good to see you, too, David.
CHRISTOPHER (*To* RICHARD) O'Donnell is the dominie in our local school and valued for a range of talents but most especially for his remarkable choir, his renowned choir.
CLEMENT Sir, I merely —
CHRISTOPHER No, no; it is the envy of every school in the kingdom.
CLEMENT The very reason for my trespass now, Mr Christopher — my choir.
CHRISTOPHER Let me get you a drink.
CLEMENT I'm already well fortified and —
CHRISTOPHER Not a bit of it.
DAVID What will it be?
MARGARET Nothing! Nothing at all! Can't you see the man's drunk already?
CLEMENT (*To* RICHARD) I am Margaret's father, Sir.

MARGARET   You'll get no drink in this house. Off you go now!

CLEMENT   But without my daughter's circumspection.

DAVID   A cup of tea, Clement! The very thing!

MARGARET *departs into the house.*

CLEMENT   And if she hadn't cut herself off from her home and her people she might recall a man of some faded nicety. And even at his present disadvantage he is alert to the nuances of a situation like this.

CHRISTOPHER   (*Silencing hand*) O'Donnell!

CLEMENT   Sir.

DAVID   What were you going to tell us about your choir?

CLEMENT   I came up to enquire did you hear us? We performed our new piece for you.

CHRISTOPHER   Today?

CLEMENT   A short time ago.

CHRISTOPHER   Missed that, O'Donnell, I'm afraid. We were away all morning at the Lifford memorial.

CLEMENT   Ah yes. Bad, bad business.

DAVID   Did you have the children out in the school yard?

CLEMENT   In splendid voice, too.

CHRISTOPHER   (*To* RICHARD) You missed a treat. They really are superb.

CLEMENT   The music liberates them briefly from their poverty, Mr Richard. A fleet and thrilling mayfly — if you're an angling man. When they sing they fashion their own ethereal opulence and become a little heavenly themselves. You'll pardon me: alcohol tends to mollify the mind.

DAVID   What's the new piece, Clement?

CLEMENT   Yet another Tom Moore, I'm afraid.

DAVID   Unison or harmony?

CLEMENT   Three-part harmony. (*To* RICHARD) I have a modest talent for harmonic arranging.

RICHARD   I do believe I did hear you.

CLEMENT You never did, Sir!

RICHARD We did, Perkins, didn't we?

PERKINS Overheard, Sir, indeed.

CLEMENT I'm so pleased.

RICHARD Far off in the distance. Yes. Very — very fetching.

CLEMENT The piece you heard was 'Oft in the Stilly Night' — (*Laughs*) — that's the title. Are you familiar with Mr Moore?

RICHARD With — ?

CLEMENT Thomas Moore, close friend of your Lord Byron.

RICHARD Not acquainted, I'm afraid.

DAVID 'The Young May Moon — '

CLEMENT ' — is beaming, love.' 'The Last Rose of Summer'?

DAVID 'Believe Me If All Those Endearing Young Charms'?

CLEMENT 'The Minstrel Boy to the War is Gone'? (*To* RICHARD) From his *Irish Melodies*.

CHRISTOPHER Where did he (*David*) pick up all those?

CLEMENT We consider him our national poet, Sir.

RICHARD Byron?

CLEMENT Tom Moore. Little Tommy Moore. Our sweet and elegant manikin. And when we lost him twenty-six years ago — to use his own image — the wind no longer blew through our sleeping harp.

RICHARD (*Totally confused. To* CHRISTOPHER) Really?

CHRISTOPHER Sorry we missed that. Will you perform for us again?

CLEMENT This evening. What about this evening?

CHRISTOPHER No, not today. Maybe next —

CLEMENT Specially for your guests. It will be my pleasure. I'll assemble my songsters in an hour's time.

CHRISTOPHER No, no, that's much too much trouble for —

CLEMENT It will be my pleasure. Just give me time to assemble my nightingales. (*Departing*) Mr Richard — Mr Perkins —

CHRISTOPHER Come back at once, O'Donnell. You're not leaving this house without some hospitality.

DAVID A sandwich, Clement? A piece of shortbread?

CLEMENT On another occasion. We will require a brief

rehearsal. Honoured to make your acquaintance.

DAVID You'll sing 'Oft in the Stilly Night' again?

CLEMENT If you wish.

DAVID Please do.

CLEMENT (*To* RICHARD) I imagine you have poets in England of much greater accomplishment, Mr Richard. But Tom Moore is the finest singer we have; the voice of our nation. Yes — yes — a romantic man and given to easy sentiment, as I am myself; a mixture of rapture and pathos. But he has our true measure, Mr Richard. He divines us accurately. He reproduces features of our history and our character. And he is an astute poet who knows that certain kinds of songs are necessary for his people. And they were especially necessary at the time he sang them.

RICHARD Good heavens.

CLEMENT Oh yes, our true measure, as I hope you'll agree when you hear us. Truer of us, I am certain, than the people who felt they had to take vengeance on the unfortunate Lord Lifford. But *sé sin scéal eile*, a *fabula alia*. Anyhow, they are both gone now, the lord and the poet. And may they both find peace.

He exits. RICHARD *bursts out laughing.*

RICHARD Well — well! What a grotesque! And the reek of whiskey off him! Or was it ether?

CHRISTOPHER Don't underestimate him. An interesting study is Clement.

RICHARD A buffoon! 'The voice of our nation' — good God!

CHRISTOPHER As he says himself, a man of some nicety.

RICHARD And he sired that delicious Margaret? That's a damned lie. Put him in a skirt and he could be a dervish, Perkins, couldn't he?

PERKINS In a skirt, Sir, indeed.

RICHARD And notice the close-set eyes and the short

arms. Certainly not native of this area, is he?

CHRISTOPHER   The O'Donnells have been here for close on two millennia.

RICHARD   Deformed by in-breeding then.

DAVID   Clement is a friend of ours, Richard, and a friend of this house.

RICHARD   Alcohol — or indeed ether — would account for the distended nostrils but not the protruding forehead. And you tell me he is a man of music?

DAVID   (*Gathering dishes*) We're all finished here, aren't we?

CHRISTOPHER   Go ahead.

RICHARD   Because very often when a specimen deviates from the physical norms of his tribe, some psychological peculiarity manifests itself, too. So a skill in music wouldn't be all that unusual. Can't have had any formal music training, our dominie, did he? Couldn't have. Must be instinctive.

CHRISTOPHER   You did make that name up, didn't you?

DAVID   What name?

CHRISTOPHER   Selberwhatever.

DAVID   No.

CHRISTOPHER   No? Remarkable.

SALLY *appears stage right.*

SALLY   There are some people here, Mr Gore.

CHRISTOPHER   Where did you find them?

SALLY   Down at the gate. They were shy about coming up.

CHRISTOPHER   Well done, little Sally! Ask them to join us.

SALLY *exits right.*

I did promise you, didn't I? And only half-an-hour behind schedule.

RICHARD   (*Wryly*) Is that all?

CHRISTOPHER   (*Calling*) Tell them we're waiting on them. Splendid! Everything's in hand.

RICHARD   (*To* PERKINS) Is everything in hand?

PERKINS Ship-shape, Sir.

RICHARD Put that instrument box on the table.

CHRISTOPHER (*Quietly, to* RICHARD) These are not sophisticated people, Dick. You will be considerate of them?

RICHARD You're twittering, Chris.

CHRISTOPHER And patient, if you would. They are my neighbours; this is my home.

RICHARD Neighbours — home — what's this sudden delicacy?

CHRISTOPHER But you will be — ?

RICHARD I'm a scientist; not a nanny.

DAVID If you need me, I'll be in the stables.

CHRISTOPHER Of course you're needed. Why is he always running away?

But DAVID *has gone round the side of the house.* SALLY *enters right.*

SALLY Here they are, Mr Gore.

CHRISTOPHER Excellent! Ask Margaret to join us. Tell her the coast's clear — her father has left. I know she's going to enjoy this. We all are. Aren't we, cousin?

Quick black.

ACT TWO

The action continues. Three people enter right slowly and cautiously, one behind the other: MARY SWEENEY, *middle-aged; very shabbily dressed; frantic, close to despair.* TOMMY BOYLE, *about fourteen; bare feet; scampish and altogether irrepressible.* MAISIE MCLAUGHLIN, *about eleven; very shy and very nervous. This environment is strange to them. They enter in a shuffling line. Only* TOMMY *is uninhibited.*

CHRISTOPHER There we are! Welcome! Welcome! Thank you kindly for coming. I do know I've thrown your routine into disarray and I do apologise. And I am most grateful. Of course I know the faces. But the names, I'm afraid, some of the names — Never mind! It will all come back presently. (*To* MARY) And how are you, my dear?

MARY I need the money, Sir, because I've —

CHRISTOPHER And you are?

MARY Mary Sweeney, Sir.

CHRISTOPHER Very good of you to come, Mary.

MARY Sir, I need the money for food for my —

CHRISTOPHER Greatly appreciated. Thank you.

MARY There's no food in the house and there's six young —

CHRISTOPHER And welcome to The Lodge. (*To* TOMMY) And who have we here?

TOMMY How are you doing, Major?

CHRISTOPHER Thank you, I am doing well. And what is your name?

TOMMY Tommy Boyle — from out beside Lough Anna.

CHRISTOPHER And a most beautiful place that is, too. And in your bare feet! Aren't you a virile chappie?

TOMMY What does that mean?

CHRISTOPHER It means you're a robustly masculine young man.

45

TOMMY　(*To all*) That doesn't sound too bad at all, does it?

CHRISTOPHER　You are, too.

TOMMY　Bejaysus that'll do me. And not a shoe on my foot!

CHRISTOPHER　And a little saucy, too, I suspect.

TOMMY　Saucy Tommy Boyle from Lough Anna! Virile Tommy Boyle from Lough Anna! Bejaysus, Major, you've the right man here for whatever the job is.

CHRISTOPHER　I'm not a major, Thomas.

TOMMY　Neither am I too. So there's a pair of us in it, isn't there?

MARGARET arrives at the French windows and watches on.

MARY　Sir, I'm a widow woman; and there's six young ones in the house; and the man's dead for over four months; and I can't —

CHRISTOPHER　We'll come to that in time, Mary. (*To* MAISIE) And you're most welcome, too. And what is your name?

What MAISIE says is inaudible.

Didn't catch that.

MARGARET　Maisie McLaughlin.

CHRISTOPHER　Welcome, Maisie McLaughlin.

TOMMY　How are you doing, Maggie? Are you rightly?

CHRISTOPHER　And look at that amazing head of curls.

TOMMY　(*To* MARGARET) It's Tommy Boyle; from Lough Anna; Thomas to you!

MARGARET　I know.

CHRISTOPHER　(*To* MARGARET) Aren't they wonderful? (*To* MAISIE) Are they natural, Maisie?

Silence.

MARGARET Don't be silly, Christopher.

TOMMY They might be natural, Major, but bejaysus they're not virile!

CHRISTOPHER (*Icily*) Yes. Splendid. Now — introductions. Dr Gore, Cousin Richard, all the way from the home place in Kent. Dr Richard is the man who is going to classify us all, ha-ha. And his assistant, Perkins. As for myself, you'll all have seen me pottering around Ballybeg over the years, haven't you? — And that's about all there is to say, isn't it — ?

> JOHNNY MACLOONE *enters right. Hand outstretched,* CHRISTOPHER *goes to meet him.*

Ah! Another volunteer! Come along, Sir. Come and join us. And welcome you are, too. Don't think I recognize the face and I should, shouldn't I? Certainly not a tenant — that I do know.

> *Silence.*

Can you assist us, Margaret?

MARGARET No.

CHRISTOPHER (*To* JOHNNY) You'll have to help me out. How did you hear about our little exercise?

> *Silence.*

RICHARD Can we get started, Chris?

CHRISTOPHER By all means. Dr Richard will explain what he proposes to do.

RICHARD No, he won't. That's Perkins' job.

TOMMY Good man, Perkins!

CHRISTOPHER (*Softly, to* RICHARD) I did promise you, didn't I? And not one of them is a tenant of mine.

RICHARD So?

CHRISTOPHER So have a little more faith, cousin.

RICHARD Twittering again, Chris. (*To* PERKINS) Carry on.

PERKINS   Sir.

RICHARD   And briefly.

PERKINS   Briefly. You will maintain your position in line until you are summoned and then you will sit in an upright position in this seat. As Dr Gore announces each measurement, I will enter it into these cards which are small enough to fit into the waistcoat pocket; and since the details of each specimen can be made by a single pencil mark, this admits of rapid and accurate use particularly in difficult field-work conditions where —

RICHARD   Perkins.

PERKINS   Sir. The instruments the doctor will use are as follows. Sliding rule. This for measuring your span or fathom. You will stand upright — thus — feet together, arms extended to full length. The measurement will then be taken from the tip of the middle finger of one hand, across the back, to the tip of the middle finger of the other hand.

TOMMY   Bejaysus, anybody can do that!

CHRISTOPHER   Please, Thomas.

TOMMY   Sorry, Major.

PERKINS   You will then sit upright in that chair. Chesterman's steel tape. This for ascertaining the horizontal circumferential of the head — or cranium. This measurement must be taken above the eyebrows to avoid distortion and round the top of both auricles — or ears. Dr Cunningham's craniometer. This — as the name implies — for measuring the cranium — or head; specifically cranial height and auriculo- and alveolar-radii. This particular craniometer is a modification of Mr Busk's original craniometer and was manufactured for us by Mr Robinson of Grafton Street in Dublin with whom you will be acquainted on your visits to —

RICHARD   Perkins.

PERKINS   Sir. Flower's anthropometer, known affection-
          ately among ourselves as the Traveller's anthro-
          pometer.

TOMMY   Flower looks like a boy could do you an injury!

PERKINS   This is for all requisite measurements except the
          cranial circumference which, as I have explained,
          is ascertained by our friend, Dr C.

CHRISTOPHER   (*Softly to* MARGARET) We misjudged him — a
          prattling parrot.

MARGARET Shhh.

RICHARD   Please.

PERKINS   Dr Gore will also take note of the colour of each
          specimen's eyes; the main classifications being
          light, medium and dark. These colours are then
          subdivided into all blue, bluish grey, light grey,
          dark brown, brownish grey, hazel, light hazel,
          hazel-grey, hazel-green, green —

RICHARD   Perkins.

PERKINS   Sir. Hair will also be noted and classified as red,
          fair, brown, dark or black. Black hair — niger —
          hence nigresence — includes not only jet-black
          but also that very intense brown which occurs
          in people who in childhood have very dark
          brown hair which in the adult cannot be distin-
          guished from coal-black except in very good
          light.

RICHARD   As today.

PERKINS   As indeed today, Sir. When everybody has been
          processed I will lead you to the yard at the rere
          of the house and there I will take a photograph,
          or image on chemical paper, of each specimen.

TOMMY   That's what has me up here! The mammy thinks
          I'm beautiful!

PERKINS   This photograph is in lieu of payment and will
          be your personal trophy. It can be picked up
          here in The Lodge in three weeks' time — if that
          is suitable for you, Mr Gore.

CHRISTOPHER   On one condition: that you take a photograph of
          Margaret here too.

MARGARET Christopher!

PERKINS My pleasure, Sir. All our computations are made in millimetres in accordance with guidelines laid down by the London Anthropological Institute; even though the Frankfurt Congress — to which most of our anthropometrist brothers subscribe — would prefer that we take our —

RICHARD Perkins.

PERKINS Sir.

RICHARD Let's commence. You first, child (*Maisie*). Yes, you — you — you.

MAISIE *is frightened and does not move.*

CHRISTOPHER Don't be nervous, Maisie. Nothing to it. Just a few measurements.

RICHARD Stand up straight as Perkins showed you. Feet together — arms wide. Don't let your hands go limp, child! Keep them parallel to the ground.

CHRISTOPHER Like this, Maisie.

TOMMY Pretend you're a scarecrow, Maisie.

RICHARD *takes the measurement efficiently and brusquely. He has done this hundreds of times.*

RICHARD That's it. (*Calls*) Span: 1670. Sit down — yes — on the chair — sit! Sit! (*Calls*) Cephalic: length — 196; breadth — 151. Lift your face. (*Calls*) Height — 127; circumference — 550.

MARGARET Good girl, Maisie.

RICHARD (*Calls*) Facial: length — 123; breadth — 137.

PERKINS Breadth — 137.

CHRISTOPHER You're doing splendidly, Maisie.

TOMMY By God she is!

RICHARD Stop fidgeting! (*Calls*) Nasal: length — 54; breadth — 31. Let's see the eyes. (*Calls*) Ocular: internal — 27; external — 88. Get to your feet. Up straight — shoulders back — body stiff.

	(*Calls*) Body height: 1660. (*Calls*) Hair: brown.
PERKINS	Hair brown.
RICHARD	(*Calls*) Eyes: hazel-grey. And that's it.
MARGARET	I love your dress, Maisie.
CHRISTOPHER	Isn't it pretty?
RICHARD	Wasn't too arduous, was it? Next!
CHRISTOPHER	Well done indeed, Maisie.
RICHARD	(*To* MARY) You're next, Madam, aren't you?
TOMMY	Take me next, boss. I'm rearing for it. Tommy Boyle's your prime man.
RICHARD	Madam, please.
CHRISTOPHER	Nothing to it, Mary. (*To* MARGARET) You know Mary Sweeney?
MARGARET	I know her people.
RICHARD	(*To* TOMMY) Get back into line.
TOMMY	Major, I —
RICHARD	(*To* MARY) Come on, Madam, come on!

MARY SWEENEY *steps forward.*

| MARY | (*Wheedling*) You'll pay me money, Sir, won't you? Just a few coppers. I'm only a widow woman. |
| RICHARD | You'll get a photograph like everybody else. Feet together — head up — shoulders back. |

CON DOHERTY *emerges from the thicket left. He stands unnoticed and watches* MARY SWEENEY *being measured.*

MARY	It's money I need, Sir.
RICHARD	(*Calls*) Span: 1703. Sit down — yes — there! Sit! Sit!
MARY	The man's dead since Easter last and I'm alone with six wee ones and it's money I need to put a crust on the —
RICHARD	Don't look at me. Look straight ahead.
TOMMY	Hold your head up, Mary, and stare at Perkins. Right, Major?
MARY	A couple of coppers is all I'm asking for, Sir, just

	to —
RICHARD	Quiet, please!
CHRISTOPHER	And you'll get them, Mary. Margaret will take care of you.
MARGARET	As soon as this is over, Mary.
RICHARD	(*Calls*) Cephalic: length — 192.
MARY	(*To* CHRISTOPHER) God bless you and yours, Sir.
RICHARD	(*Calls*) Breadth — 148; height — 131.
MARY	(*To* CHRISTOPHER) You were always a —
RICHARD	Quiet! (*Calls*) Circumference — 554.
PERKINS	554.
RICHARD	(*To* CHRISTOPHER) I never told you, did I, that I once saw a Brahmin widow commit suttee. (*Calls*) Facial: length — 134; breadth — 139. Yes, way up in the foothills west of Calcutta. A typhoid epidemic in our station there and I went up to give them a hand. (*Calls*) Nasal: length — 51; breadth — 33. Astonishing sight, the suttee business.
PERKINS	Sorry, Sir. Breadth?
TOMMY	33, Perkins.
RICHARD	First she distributed her jewels to the assembled mourners. Then, when her husband's funeral pyre is blazing away merrily — keep your arms still! — up she scrambles to the very top of it, nimble as a goat, and immolates herself! Astonishing!
TOMMY	Bejaysus, you wouldn't get a Lough Anna woman to do that!
RICHARD	(*Calls*) Ocular: internal — 30; external — 91. Whole grizzly spectacle lasted — what? — maybe half-an-hour.
MARY	(*To* CHRISTOPHER) Or if you had any old clothes, Sir —
RICHARD	And the amazing thing is she never uttered a sound. (*Tweaks* MARY's *ear playfully*) You could learn a thing from her, couldn't you? We banned the bizarre custom fifty years ago but it persists in a few remote areas still.

MARY (*To* CHRISTOPHER) If you had an old shirt or jacket, Sir —

CHRISTOPHER Certainly — certainly — a pleasure.

RICHARD Get to your feet. Up — up — up! Not a whimper out of her. Drugged to the eyes with cannabis, I imagine. Had no idea what was happening. (*Calls*) Height: 1702. Who will climb up on your pyre, Christopher? (*Calls*) Hair: brown. Eyes: light grey. Next!

CHRISTOPHER Well done, Mary. Talk to Margaret before you leave.

MARY God bless you and yours, Sir. God reward you as you deserve.

RICHARD You, boy!

TOMMY *steps forward.*

TOMMY You have the best of them now, boss.

RICHARD Have I indeed?

TOMMY They don't come any better than the virile Tommy Boyle. Set him before a six-foot wall and Tommy'll clear it from standing still.

CHRISTOPHER *now sees* CON.

CHRISTOPHER Ah — another volunteer, Richard! Excellent! Welcome! Now that's a face I do know. What a wonderful turn-out! Michael Doherty — am I right?

CON Almost, Mr Gore. Not Michael; Con; Con Doherty.

RICHARD (*To* TOMMY) Arms out wide. Hands straight.

CHRISTOPHER From the cottages behind Roarty's forge? Of course!

RICHARD (*Calls*) Span: 1513.

CON And how are you, Maggie?

MARGARET (*Icily*) Well.

CON Haven't seen you for ages. (*To* CHRISTOPHER) Maggie and I are cousins, you know.

CHRISTOPHER I think I know that, don't I? Another specimen,

	Dick.
RICHARD	Yes? (*Calls*) Cephalic: length — 186.
CHRISTOPHER	(*To* RICHARD) A friend from below in Ballybeg.
CON	That's young Tommy Boyle, isn't it?
TOMMY	Hello, Con. The virile Tommy Boyle in person.
RICHARD	Quiet! (*Calls*) Breadth — 153.
PERKINS	Breadth again, Sir?
TOMMY	153.

RICHARD Pay attention, Perkins. (*Raps* TOMMY's *head sharply with his knuckles*) Stop looking round, boy.

TOMMY Sorry, boss.

CHRISTOPHER (*To* CON) My cousin, Dr Gore.

CON I know.

CHRISTOPHER Richard is an anthropologist, if you don't mind — or an ethnologist — or whatever. *You* know, Margaret.

MARGARET What do you want up here?

CON You're looking well, Maggie.

RICHARD Head up. (*Calls*) Height — 130; circumference — 587. You are a big-headed boy, you are.

TOMMY That's Tommy, boss! You need a big head for these brains.

CON Ask your cousin to stop that, Mr Gore.

CHRISTOPHER Sorry?

CON Tell him to stop that. There's been enough of this.

CHRISTOPHER Enough of what? I'm not sure what —

CON It must stop now. Tell him.

CHRISTOPHER (*Laughs*) Now, now, Con —

CON We have no quarrel with you, Mr Gore. But I'm not going to say this again. Tell your cousin to pack his things and leave. Himself and his assistant.

CHRISTOPHER I'm afraid I'll do no —

CON Immediately. Get to your feet, Tommy.

TOMMY *gets to his feet.*

RICHARD Who is this — ?

CON   Good boy. Off you go home.

TOMMY   I want my picture taken!

CON   Do as you're told, Tommy.

TOMMY   The mammy expects me to come back with —

CON   At once.

RICHARD   Who is this, Chris?

CON   You, too, Maisie. Off you go. (*Claps his hands*) Smartly!

MAISIE *and* TOMMY *run off.*

CHRISTOPHER   Hold on, Sir. This is a little insolent. Nobody's going anywhere. (*Calls*) Maisie — Tommy —

CON   You, too, Mary. Home. Off with you.

MARY   You promised me a few coppers, Mr Gore. You did.

CON   And you'll get them. I'll call on you later this evening. Away you go now.

MARY *leaves.*

CHRISTOPHER   I don't know what you think you're doing. But this is a perfectly innocuous survey. And this is my home. And you are trespassing.

CON   I'm not trespassing, Mr Gore. (*To* RICHARD) You two — pick up your belongings and get out of here.

MARGARET   How dare you speak like that to our guests, you little —

CHRISTOPHER   I'll deal with this, Margaret.

RICHARD   Allow me. (*To* CON) I have no idea who you are or what your purpose is. But I know an insolent pup when I see one. And if you don't leave immediately I'll have you flung in prison.

CHRISTOPHER   Perhaps we're all getting a little —

RICHARD   Throw him out, Perkins.

PERKINS   Sir.

MARGARET   Where's David? I'll get David! Oh my God! Wait until David comes!

She rushes off. PERKINS *moves towards* CON. JOHNNY MACLOONE *steps in front of him.*

PERKINS (*To* JOHNNY) Now, Sir, why don't you just step —
JOHNNY No further, mister. You've gone far enough.

JOHNNY *produces a cudgel from under his jacket.*

CON No, no, put that away, Johnny. Nobody wants this to end in a brawl. These men are going to leave now. (*Calls*) Sally!
RICHARD (*To* CHRISTOPHER) This creature's a tenant of yours? Is this how your tenants behave?
CON No need for raised voices. Just pick up your things and leave.
RICHARD Are you going to allow this highwayman to insult you and defy you?
CHRISTOPHER Let's all keep calm.
RICHARD In the presence of that?
CHRISTOPHER I understood you came here as a volunteer. I now suspect you are here to make a political gesture; to indicate to Richard and me that — for some reason that makes no sense whatever to me — for some reason you object to Dr Gore carrying out his scientific research. You have made your protest. And now I must ask you to — to simply withdraw and we'll forget that this episode ever took place.

SALLY *enters.*

SALLY You called me, Con?
CON These men are leaving. Would you bring their bags down?
SALLY Bring their bags down. Certainly, Sir.

She exits.

CHRISTOPHER Very well then. In that case I demand, Michael,

that you —

CON Con, Mr Gore.

CHRISTOPHER This is my house. And you are an intruder —

RICHARD A damned thug!

CHRISTOPHER And I order you off my property immediately.

CON There are three men down at the foot of the avenue, Mr Gore. They wanted to come up here with me but I persuaded them to wait down there.

RICHARD Chris, don't remonstrate any more with —

CON They'll wait there to make sure your guests leave. If they don't see your guests leave those three men will come up here.

PERKINS (*To* RICHARD) Sir, do you want me to — ?

CHRISTOPHER These are my guests! This is my home! And we will not be intimidated by you or your shadowy friends.

CON You're not being helpful, Mr Gore.

CHRISTOPHER I've had a bellyful of this. I know very well who you are, Doherty, and I know something about your dubious activities and I assure you this behaviour won't go unpunished.

CON I've told you — we have no quarrel with you, Sir. All we ask is that these men leave.

CHRISTOPHER And they will not leave! No, Sir, they will not leave!

CON You don't know the men down at the gates, Mr Gore. Temperate men in normal times; but they find this measuring business offensive — as I do myself.

SALLY *returns.*

SALLY They're in the hall, Con.

CON Thank you. (*To* CHRISTOPHER) One of the men you might know of: he has suddenly acquired some little fame — notoriety maybe — around here. And all because a fistful of hair was pulled out of his head — from just here — exactly four

57

weeks ago today.

DAVID *and* MARGARET *emerge from the house.*

	Good afternoon, David.
DAVID	What's the trouble, Con? Is something the matter?
CON	I don't think there is any trouble — is there?
RICHARD	Help us fling this bully out, David.
MARGARET	Do something, David. You have got to step in here.
DAVID	What's the matter, Father?
CHRISTOPHER	There was a misunderstanding that has now been —
RICHARD	This bully has threatened us.
CHRISTOPHER	Has now been sorted out. Everything's in hand.
MARGARET	Christopher, for God's sake —
RICHARD	I have never witnessed a more disgraceful situation: an entire household being intimidated by two peasant cut-throats.
CHRISTOPHER	Please — please — please. Language like that is no help at all. Everything's in hand.
RICHARD	Everything's out of hand, for Christ's sake!
MARGARET	He's right, Chris. Stand up to him. This is your home.
CHRISTOPHER	Pay attention to me — Richard — Margaret — everybody. Thank you. One minute, please. Thank you. This discussion has —
RICHARD	Discussion?
CHRISTOPHER	This discussion will now end. I have listened with attention to both sides and I have now decided that what is going to happen — in the best interests of all of us — what must happen is this. Cousin Richard and his assistant will leave immediately. Their work here is complete. If they make reasonable progress they will be well on their way to Galway before dark. This is best for all. Their work here is finished.
RICHARD	Are you betraying me, Christopher?
CON	Mr Gore is being sensible.

MARGARET Christopher, you're not going to —

CHRISTOPHER (*Angrily*) Keep out of this! Nothing at all to do with you, Margaret!

MARGARET You coward.

CHRISTOPHER My decision only. There's nothing more to say. Everything's in hand.

MARGARET David, can *you* not — ?

CHRISTOPHER Bring their bags out here, Sally.

DAVID Why are you doing this, Father?

RICHARD You are a traitor, Christopher.

CON (*To* DAVID) Your guests aren't welcome around here and your father has decided that they should leave now.

DAVID Is that true, Father?

CON And he has made the right decision. Oh, yes, he has. (*To* CHRISTOPHER) You know you've made the right decision, Mr Gore, don't you?

Light change. A couple of hours have passed. The lawn is furnished as before. CHRISTOPHER *is sitting outside, his face raised, his eyes resolutely closed, his body rigid.* MARGARET *comes in to the breakfast room with a handful of bills and receipts. She goes to the escritoire and busies herself comparing these papers with the receipts in the desk.*

MARGARET This man is becoming more and more brazen every week. You must do something about him, Christopher. He pays no attention to me.

CHRISTOPHER (*Not listening*) Must I?

MARGARET Sugar is now three pence a pound. Last week it was tuppence. This week tea is three shillings. Last week two-and-six.

> *She comes out to the lawn with the bills in her hand.*

And look at this. Paraffin oil and candles: one pound fourteen. That would light the whole place for three months. This is the only house he's fleecing and he mustn't get away with it. A real swindler is O'Farrell.

CHRISTOPHER 'A real swindler is O'Farrell.' Don't you people say, 'O'Farrell is a real swindler'?

Brief pause.

MARGARET Bacon — seven-and-six. He's a robber! You could buy a whole side of bacon for that. And his father was a decent man. I remember him well. He used to come round selling herring from his handcart; and he'd park just across the street from the school; and he'd chant, 'Herring! Fresh herring! Fresh herring make you strong.' And if he had any fish left at the end of the day he'd just give them away. And we scrambled and fought among ourselves to get one. The great trophy — a stiff and stinking herring — we were thrilled! (*Laughs*) He was known locally as Fish O'Farrell.

CHRISTOPHER Very inventive.

Pause.

MARGARET There was another old man I remember, too. Sold buttermilk from a huge wooden churn in the back of his cart. What was his name? Cannon? Canning? Anyhow. The tricks we used to play on that old huckster. One of us would have the job of distracting him: maybe tell him his horse was lame or the wheel of his cart was cracked. And when he'd be examining it, the most daring of us — the cheekiest of us — would creep on to the back of the cart and turn the tap of the churn full on. Then we'd bolt like rabbits round the corner and watch the flood of buttermilk pour down the street; laughing our heads off and terrified at the same time. Bad monkeys, weren't we?

For the first time CHRISTOPHER *opens his eyes.*

CHRISTOPHER Sorry — what's that?
MARGARET I do think you should take this business in hand yourself (*bills*).
CHRISTOPHER 'I do think — ' Proper little English woman today is Miss O'Donnell, isn't she?
MARGARET Why are you being so — ?
CHRISTOPHER And am I required to examine them just now? At this very minute?

She goes back quickly to the breakfast room and busies herself at the desk. He follows her immediately.

Forgive me — I'm on edge — I'm sorry.
MARGARET We can go over them another day.
CHRISTOPHER I'm still in shock.
MARGARET I know.
CHRISTOPHER Do you?

She moves away from him. He looks at his watch.

I've decided to ask Penny over for the weekend.
MARGARET Yes.
CHRISTOPHER Show solidarity with the tribe.
MARGARET Why not.
CHRISTOPHER And get her out of that damned mausoleum for a couple of nights.
MARGARET Good idea.
CHRISTOPHER Lucy loved having her over, rest in peace. We both did. Pert and intrepid Penny Pasco. She really must detest that damned place now.
MARGARET You should do that.

He looks at his watch again. Pause.

CHRISTOPHER They could have got the length of Sligo by now. Spend the night with Colonel Harvey maybe — Of course he'll never forgive me, Richard. How could he ever — ? You're right: I am a coward.

MARGARET We were all cowardly.

CHRISTOPHER And of course there is a list.

MARGARET (*Firmly*) We are not going to go back over that again. There is no list. Doherty was very explicit. They have no quarrel with you, he said.

CHRISTOPHER I should be grateful to your cousin then, should I?

MARGARET But you have got to report the whole episode to the police.

CHRISTOPHER Was there an episode?

MARGARET For God's sake, man: threats, trespass, intimidation. You just can't ignore all that.

He shrugs.

You must talk to the Sergeant, Christopher.

He goes to the French windows and stands looking out over the countryside.

Are you listening to me? At least have a private word with him.

Long pause.

CHRISTOPHER I can't tell you how beautiful the home place is at this time of year. And how tranquil. And how — replete. The orchards; and the deer park; and the lines of bee-hives in the pampered walled garden; and the great placid fields of wheat and oats and barley. A golden and beneficent land. Days without blemish. Every young man's memory, isn't it? — or fiction? — or whatever.

Your father hasn't a monopoly on romance and easy sentiment. I'm an exile from both that memory and this fact now, amn't I?

MARGARET Christopher, this is your home.

Pause.

CHRISTOPHER (*With sudden and feigned enthusiasm*) So we rise above, don't we? Isn't that what we do?

SALLY *enters. She carries her belongings in a paper bag.*

Wasn't that splendid advice, Sally?

SALLY What was that, Sir?

CHRISTOPHER My father's only bequest on me. Well, this (*house*) too; but this is a treacherous legacy. 'Rise above' — should be on the family crest of every planter, shouldn't it?

SALLY I wouldn't know that, Mr Gore.

CHRISTOPHER Indeed you would, you sly little puss.

SALLY I'm off now, Sir.

CHRISTOPHER What do you mean?

MARGARET I've asked her to leave.

CHRISTOPHER What's all this, Margaret?

SALLY Off home, Sir.

MARGARET We both think it's better.

CHRISTOPHER We haven't offended you in some way, have we?

SALLY You, Sir? Never! But Maggie's right: it is better. And haven't I tormented you long enough? And I'll be getting married soon anyway.

CHRISTOPHER We have offended you, Sally, haven't we? Because if we have —

SALLY You've always been a gentleman. I'll miss you and The Lodge.

CHRISTOPHER And we'll miss you sadly. Who'll keep me on my toes now?

SALLY And if you ever need me for a few days, just send down for me — especially if Mr Perkins is here.

CHRISTOPHER You and Perkins — of course! Very smitten was Mr Perkins.

SALLY I know, Sir. How did he escape? Have I lost the touch?

MARGARET Off you go now.

CHRISTOPHER And you're getting married! Congratulations! Soon, is it?

SALLY I'm doing my best to hustle him, Sir. But he's a bit of a slug.

CHRISTOPHER (*Laughs*) Bit of a slug!

SALLY (*To* MARGARET) I've changed the sheets and the towels. And the curtains are steeping in a bucket at the back door. And the potatoes are in a saucepan on the range. And I washed the pantry windows.

MARGARET Thank you.

SALLY And I've locked up the chickens. (*To* CHRISTOPHER) The falcon's back.

CHRISTOPHER Really?

SALLY Goodbye, Mr Gore.

CHRISTOPHER Sweet child, goodbye. All these sudden departures — I'm bereft.

He fumbles in his pockets, produces a note and thrusts it into her hand.

Here — here — here — put that in your pocket.

SALLY Mr Gore, I couldn't —

CHRISTOPHER To please me.

SALLY Maggie gave me my money.

CHRISTOPHER I do insist. Buy yourself a parasol and silk gloves.

SALLY No, no, Sir. I can't take money from —

MARGARET Take it.

SALLY Well — Thank you, Mr Gore. You were always a kind and generous man.

MARGARET Off you go. And keep in touch with us.

SALLY Say goodbye to David for me. Thank you again, Sir. 'Bye.

She goes off right.

CHRISTOPHER That's unexpected, isn't it?

MARGARET I'm not sure if she can be depended on.

CHRISTOPHER Little Sally? She's a wonderful worker. And she's engaged? Who's the young gentleman?

MARGARET Local man, I think.

CHRISTOPHER I just hope he's worthy of her. She'll bring a lot of joy into any house.

MARGARET I imagine they're well matched. Do you want me to look out for someone to replace her now? It would be easier to get somebody after the harvest.

CHRISTOPHER Get somebody right away if you can. You can't manage all this on your own.

He takes her hand.

MARGARET If that's what you want.

CHRISTOPHER You know what I want.

MARGARET Please, Christopher.

CHRISTOPHER (*Suddenly, rapidly*) Let's go away. Leave all this behind. Make a life somewhere else — Africa, South America, India — anywhere where roles aren't imposed on us — where we'll be free of history and heritage and the awful burden of this (*house*).

MARGARET Christopher —

CHRISTOPHER You know how I feel about you. I've never made a secret of it. I want to marry you, Margaret.

MARGARET This is not the day to —

CHRISTOPHER You choose where we'll go.

MARGARET We're not going anywhere.

CHRISTOPHER You're an exile here, too.

MARGARET This is my home, Christopher.

CHRISTOPHER I know — I do know — that I'm much older than you. But for whatever years are left to me. And I can't die here, Margaret.

MARGARET I know how distressing today was for you. I understand all that.

CHRISTOPHER I —

MARGARET But this has got to stop. Altogether.

CHRISTOPHER Will you marry me?

MARGARET There can be no question of marriage — no question at all.

CHRISTOPHER We'll wait until —

MARGARET So let it all end now.

CHRISTOPHER I'll ask you again in a few —

MARGARET Don't. That's final. For both our sakes.

CHRISTOPHER I'm not going to give up until —

MARGARET Final, Christopher. No. Please. (*Pause*) Listen to me: I'll go away if that would help. I mean that. I have a cousin in Boston, a dressmaker. She wants me to join her. If that would be a help, I'd go to Boston. Willingly. (*Pause*) I'm a very good dressmaker.

CHRISTOPHER A drink is needed, I believe. Will you have something?

MARGARET Nothing.

He goes into the breakfast room: gets a drink; comes outside again.

CHRISTOPHER Lifford's memorial was *this* morning, wasn't it? I'm confused. Seems like days ago. I felt no grief, I can tell you. Always hated his swagger and his shouting. He bellowed at people as if they couldn't hear him. Maybe they didn't. That's how a landlord had to behave, he believed; as do most of the huddled eleven that turned up for the service. Always knew they were wrong. And believed I could do things differently. I would be the good landlord as well as being the good neighbour and the friend-in-need when the need arose. Fell flat on my face, didn't I?

MARGARET That is not true. You are a very good landlord. You hear how warmly Father spoke of the Gores

66

and The Lodge.

CHRISTOPHER Polite sounds. A mime without meaning. Verbal gestures that just seem to indicate courtesy and deference and even warmth. But we don't share a language. You heard what I said to Sally? Buy yourself a parasol and silk gloves! Yes! And even as I said it I was aware of how alien I sounded and how absurd she found me. You see — I *do* know. I always know. It's David, isn't it? (*Pause*) It *is* David?

MARGARET I was going to tell you when —

CHRISTOPHER Yes, it's David. Of course it's David.

MARGARET I'm sorry, Christopher.

CHRISTOPHER No, no, I understand. You were always a practical woman. Circumspect — isn't that how your father described you?

MARGARET You make me sound like —

CHRISTOPHER No, no, I congratulate you. I do. So for the first time in — what? — four hundred years a Gore is going to marry out? Sounds like a schism, doesn't it? Thank God you kept that information from Cousin Richard — a 'generous infusion' of Celtic blood would have terrified him. So it's David and Margaret Gore of The Lodge? Should be a consolation for an ageing father, shouldn't it? You do know he's a little immature in some respects? 'Course you do — taken all that into your considerations. And the two of you will be so much more efficient at all of this than I ever was — or Father — or even the formidable Grandfather Gore. Your local knowledge will be invaluable. You'll be able to identify all those tenants who are lazy or unfaithful or treacherous.

MARGARET We won't have to measure their heads then?

CHRISTOPHER Indeed you'll be able to alert him to all those relatives of yours who are scheming to repossess this place and drive us out, won't you? — Oh Jesus Christ, forgive me, Margaret — I am so sorry — I don't mean a word of that — not a syllable — I'm just devastated — Oh my God, I do apologise — I'm as demented as Penny Pasco — Forgive me — So sorry — I am so sorry, Margaret.

MARGARET Listen to me, Christopher. I promise you — if all this makes life here too difficult for you — I promise you I'll leave.

CHRISTOPHER That was disgraceful. Please forgive me.

MARGARET Tell me now if it makes things impossible for you.

CHRISTOPHER No, no, I'm fine. I'll be —

MARGARET I will go — I promise.

CHRISTOPHER No, no; just give me a little time; I'll rise above. The planter has to be resilient, hasn't he? No home, no country, a life of isolation and resentment. So he has to — resile. Just give me a little time. And that resentment will stalk him — and never forget it — down through the next generation and the next and the next. The doomed nexus of those who believe themselves the possessors and those who believe they're dispossessed. Am I forgiven?

MARGARET (Gently) Christopher.

CHRISTOPHER (Quick laugh) When you and David take over, will you do something for me? Don't make it too obvious that I should die off immediately?

MARGARET For God's sake, Mr Gore! It's getting chilly. Better tidy up out here.

DAVID (Off) Father? Where are you?

CHRISTOPHER Yes?

DAVID *enters round the side of the house. He has a brush and a bucket of white-wash.*

DAVID Have you a moment now?

CHRISTOPHER I do believe I have a moment, don't I?

DAVID I have all the equipment here.

CHRISTOPHER Well done. What are you talking about?

DAVID The white-wash and the brush.

CHRISTOPHER Brush?

MARGARET Stop that, Christopher! You said you were going to mark out the trees you want cut down.

CHRISTOPHER The doomed trees! Of course! Let's do that rightaway. Hold on a second — there used to be an old record of all that planting in here somewhere —

He searches in a bookshelf in the breakfast room. MARGARET *begins tidying up the furnishings on the lawn.* DAVID *goes to her and attempts to embrace her.*

DAVID I love you.

MARGARET David.

DAVID I love you inordinately. I love you hopelessly.

MARGARET *extricates herself.*

MARGARET Not now.

DAVID And I'm going to tell him straight out that we are getting married. The days of bullying are over. Tonight. After dinner.

He attempts to embrace her again.

MARGARET I said not now, David.

DAVID You'll be at my side; you'll speak up, too, won't you?

MARGARET Marriage is not to be mentioned. Is that clear?

DAVID But we agreed that —

MARGARET You will not mention marriage tonight, David. Do you understand me?

DAVID I thought you —

MARGARET Is that perfectly clear? Not tonight — not for a month — not for twelve months.

DAVID Maggie —

MARGARET And you're spilling that damned white-wash all

over your shoes.

CHRISTOPHER *emerges with faded record.*

CHRISTOPHER Knew it was here! Should be a date somewhere — Yes, February 14, 1779.

MARGARET The year Tom Moore was born.

CHRISTOPHER In Grandfather Gore's formidable handwriting. Ninety-nine years ago!

DAVID I think we should begin behind the stables.

CHRISTOPHER So detailed and so efficient and so — just so damned beautiful. Weren't they a marvellous people! Look! Where the trees were bought — carriage costs — dates of planting of each species — record of height after six months, twelve months, five years! — failure rate in numbers and percentages — the elm were a disaster — seven per cent survival.

DAVID The soil's too alkaline for elm.

CHRISTOPHER Do you think so? And look: a separate record of specimen trees; each planted apart from any other tree; original country of origin; colour and shape of leaf; estimated root-depth. And every name in English and Latin: Maidenhair Tree — *Ginkgo biloba*; Honey Locust — *Cleditsia triacanthos*; Japanese Cedar — *Cryptomeria japonica*.

DAVID I think we should begin behind the stables.

CHRISTOPHER We'll begin where the wall of the walled garden has collapsed. First thing is to identify the specimens. They'll be distinctive. And they'll need most space. Any tree that encroaches on their territory will have to go.

DAVID Do you want to do the marking?

CHRISTOPHER I'll identify the specimens. I'll leave the artistic work to you.

MARGARET Dinner'll be in an hour's time.

CHRISTOPHER We'll be round the side of the house here.

They both go round the side of the house. DAVID

returns for a second.

DAVID (*Whispers*) Maggie — Maggie —

She ignores him and busies herself with tidying up.

CHRISTOPHER Let's begin with these. They're blocking the light in the kitchen. Mark that. And that. And that.

DAVID What about this one?

CHRISTOPHER What is it?

DAVID A sycamore. Doesn't look very healthy.

CHRISTOPHER Mark it. Ah — here's a specimen. According to Grandfather Gore it is a — yes, a walnut. That's a walnut, isn't it?

DAVID Is it?

CHRISTOPHER A *Juglans nigra*, yes! A nigrescent juglans! Needs a lot more light. Put a mark on that one that's crowding in on it.

DAVID And this?

CHRISTOPHER No, leave that.

DAVID It's an old sycamore. Doesn't look very strong.

CHRISTOPHER It looks fine to me.

DAVID It's weak-looking. I'll mark it.

CHRISTOPHER Careful, David: you don't want to denude the place altogether.

DAVID Gone.

CHRISTOPHER Don't be so harsh. Let's stick with this plan.

Their voices fade. Occasionally we hear a word or two. Now in the far distance we hear the school choir singing 'Oft in the Stilly Night'.

The moment the music begins MARGARET stands motionless, enraptured, as she did at the beginning of the play. But on this occasion for only a very short time. Then, very deliberately, she turns her back to the music and stands still. But the siren sound seduces her again. She turns round. She is drawn towards the singing

71

as she was before and drifts downstage towards it. She drops into a seat and sits there mesmerized, absorbing, submitting, remembering.
CHRISTOPHER *emerges from the thicket left.*

CHRISTOPHER Now, according to the old man, there should be a birch somewhere about — here? And indeed there is! 'Brought home by Cousin Edward from Kenya.' That's a white birch-bark, isn't it? 'A five-foot *Betula pendula tristis.*' A sad birch. (*To tree*) Why are you sad? Still hankering after Kenya? Give Cousin Edward breathing space. So — mark that and that and — David? Where are you, David?

DAVID *now emerges round the side of the house.*

DAVID Sorry. Ran out of white-wash.
CHRISTOPHER Mark that. And that.
DAVID This one, too?
CHRISTOPHER Steady on. You're being ruthless.
DAVID Marked.
CHRISTOPHER Please, David. Just do as I say.
DAVID It won't be missed.
CHRISTOPHER Now if we keep faith with the formidable Grandfather, there has to be a *Tilia americana* somewhere here. And there the lime tree is. Bravo, Grandfather!
DAVID No, that's a linden, Father.
CHRISTOPHER Linden — lime tree. Same thing, David. We'll take his word on the *americana* part. So — give him space to live. Mark that — and that. And maybe that scrubby thing should —

DAVID *points excitedly to the sky.*

DAVID Look, Father! — Look! — Look!
CHRISTOPHER What are you — ?
DAVID The falcon! There! Look — the falcon!

CHRISTOPHER I see no —
DAVID Right above your head! Quick! There!

> DAVID, *brush in hand, swings round excitedly to point to the bird. As he does, he splashes a large white-wash mark across* CHRISTOPHER's *chest and the faded record.*

CHRISTOPHER (*In a rage*) For Christ's sake! What are you — ?
DAVID Sorry — sorry — sorry —
CHRISTOPHER Look what you've done!
DAVID I was only showing you —
CHRISTOPHER You've destroyed the record, too! Jesus, what sort of a dolt are you?
DAVID I was just —
CHRISTOPHER For God's sake, go and get me a clean shirt! Look at the mess!
DAVID A what?
CHRISTOPHER A shirt — a shirt! Are you deaf, too?
DAVID Sorry, Father. I didn't mean —
CHRISTOPHER Stop mouthing! Go and get me clean clothes!
DAVID I'm sorry. I really am —
CHRISTOPHER And stop apologising! Oh, for God's sake —

> DAVID *dashes into the house.* MARGARET, *absorbed in the music and in her own memories, has been unaware of this commotion.* CHRISTOPHER *goes to where she is sitting. This is the final straw. He is on the verge of breakdown. His resilience is spent.*

CHRISTOPHER Look at the mess I'm in, Maggie. Look at what that damned fool did to me. For God's sake —
MARGARET Sit down beside me.
CHRISTOPHER He tells me there's a falcon up in the trees and the moment I look up he lashes out at me.

> *Her mood unbroken, she calmly wipes his hand with a napkin.*

MARGARET   No harm has been done.

CHRISTOPHER   There probably isn't a falcon. The oaf only imagined it. Where is he, Maggie? What's keeping him? Why is he trying to humiliate me?

MARGARET   Shhh.

CHRISTOPHER   He wants me out of the house, doesn't he? That's his plan, isn't it, Maggie?

MARGARET   Shhh.

CHRISTOPHER   Of course it's his plan. Of course there's an ugly scheme abroad. Maybe he's in cahoots with that gang that murdered poor old Lifford. Maybe they're plotting out there already. Maybe the whole of Ballybeg is going to rise up and —

He breaks down totally, she puts a comforting arm around his shoulder.

MARGARET   Shhh.

CHRISTOPHER   Oh my God, Maggie —

MARGARET   Shhh.

She rocks him.

CHRISTOPHER   I'm shattered, Maggie. I'm in total confusion. I really don't think —

MARGARET   Please.

He reaches out and catches her hand.

CHRISTOPHER   Don't think I'm able to rise above any more.

MARGARET   'Course you can.

CHRISTOPHER   Or ever again. Can't, Maggie — I can't.

MARGARET   Yes, you can. That's what we all do.

CHRISTOPHER   Not able any more. Resilience is exhausted, Maggie.

MARGARET   Shhh.

CHRISTOPHER   Help me, Maggie, will you?

DAVID *enters the breakfast room. He sees them*

in their gauche embrace. He stands at the French
windows and watches them.

MARGARET Listen to the music. Pay attention to the music.
CHRISTOPHER You don't resent me, do you?
MARGARET Sit quiet and listen.
CHRISTOPHER I know you won't betray me, Maggie. I know that.
MARGARET Don't talk. Listen. Pay attention to the music.
CHRISTOPHER Maggie —
MARGARET Shhh. Just listen. Because in a short time Father will come up here for me. Shhh.

They sit in silence and listen to the music which
soon ends. Slow fade.

Anthropometry in Aran.

Extract from
Studies in Irish Craniology: The Aran Islands, Co. Galway
by Professor A C Haddon

Read before the Royal Irish Academy on December 12, 1892.

C) INSTRUMENTS USED

We took with us 'The Traveller's Anthropometer', a very compact and useful instrument designed by Dr J G Garson and manufactured by Messrs Aston & Mander, 25, Old Compton-Street, London. This instrument is described in 'Notes and Queries on Anthropology', Second Edition (1892), published by the Anthropological Institute. It is possible to take all the requisite measurements with this instrument, except the cranial circumference, but we preferred to use other instruments for the head measurements.

We also had with us Flower's Craniometer (made by Stanley, Great Turnstile, Holborn, London), which is a very convenient instrument for this class of measurements; a compass d'épaisseur and a compass glissière (both made by Mathieu, 113, Boulevard Saint-Germain, Paris). The former is very useful for face measurements as the rounded points of the callipers reduce any danger from accidents to a minimum. The sole objection to our instrument is that it is graduated in two millimetres, and not in single millimetres. The compass glissière is a very handy and delicate little instrument, but it can be dispensed with when a Flower's Craniometer is used.

A sliding rule, such as was first used in Galton's Anthropometrical Laboratory, for measuring the span, was usually carried with our other apparatus. It is a little more convenient than adapting Garson's Anthropometer. Chesterman's steel tape was used for taking the horizontal circumference of the head.

Lastly, we measured the cranial height, and auriculo-nasal and alveolar radii, with Dr Cunningham's modification of Busk's Craniometer, made by Robinson, Grafton-Street, Dublin, an instrument which has been used in our Laboratory since its inception.[1]

All measurements were taken in millimetres.

The height of the head would best be taken from the ear-hole to the bregma, but in the vast majority of living subjects it is impossible to determine this spot. The measurement we took is convenient, and sufficiently definite.

The horizontal circumference was not taken round the eyebrows, but above them; it is very difficult to take a satisfactory measurement by the former method, owing to the tape slipping, and the variable development of the eyebrows.

The auriculo-radii were found to be readily taken in field-work; and none of the subjects measured absolutely objected to having the plugs of the instrument inserted into their ear-holes, although some demurred at first. Of 293 persons who have been measured in the Dublin Anthropometric Laboratory none have objected to the instrument being used. We thus already have a large series of the three measurements for which this instrument is employed. It is necessary in using this instrument to feel that it is actually pressing against the bony wall of the external auditory meatus.

The internal bi-ocular breadth we consider to be a valuable measurement, as giving the distance between the eyes. The external bi-ocular breadth was taken so as to give some idea as to the size of the eyes, but we did not find this of much practical value, and we consider it preferable to measure from the middle of the outer border of the one orbit to the corresponding point of the other.

The span, or fathom, is an interesting measurement and one readily made. We do not propose to discontinue this measurement, but it is worth bearing in mind that it is of little real scientific value, as it is a composite one, being the addition for four variables, viz. the hand, fore-arm, upper-arm, and the width of the body across the shoulders. In the laboratory, and in this expedition, we measure the lengths of the right hand (tip of mid-finger to styloid) and of the right fore-arm (styloid to epicondyle). It is also the custom in the laboratory to measure the right upper-arm (epicondyle to acromion), but this was found to be impossible in the case of the Aran islanders on account of the thickness of their flannel sleeves. In the laboratory, also, there is great difficulty, and sometimes it is impossible, to take this measurement. When these three upper-limb measurements can be taken, the span measurement is of considerable value. These measurements, however, can only be taken by an observer who has had some anatomical instruction, and often they are very difficult to take even by a skilled observer.

E) PHOTOGRAPHY

A considerable number of photographs were obtained of the people. In some cases groups were taken, but full-face and side-view portraits were secured of thirteen of the subjects we measured. We found that the promise of a copy of their photograph was usually a sufficient reward for undergoing the trouble of being measured and photographed.

[1] *Cf.Proc. Roy.Irish.Acad. (3), II., 1892, p.397.*

Reproduced from Proceedings of the Royal Irish Academy, Volume 18, 1892, by kind permission of the Academy.